MW00331078

Introducing Romans

Introducing Romans

Paul Jeon

WIPF & STOCK · Eugene, Oregon

INTRODUCING ROMANS

Copyright © 2011 Paul Jeon. All rights reserved. Except for brief
quotations in critical publications or reviews, no part of this book
may be reproduced in any manner without prior written permission
from the publisher. Write: Permissions, Wipf and Stock Publishers,
199 W. 8th Ave., Suite 3, Eugene, OR 97401.

Wipf & Stock
An Imprint of Wipf and Stock Publishers
199 W. 8th Ave., Suite 3
Eugene, OR 97401

www.wipfandstock.com

ISBN 13: 978-1-61097-356-4

Manufactured in the U.S.A.

Contents

Foreword

THE BOOK of Romans . . . even the mere mention of it can conjure up a sense of awe. Unfortunately, this sense of awe often leads to a sense of defeat. For those of us considering a personal study, we wonder how we could even begin to study this book. For those of us planning a class or group study for our church, we contemplate whether it would take years to study Romans properly. While we read about the effect Romans has had on giants of the faith throughout history—from St. Augustine to Martin Luther to John Calvin—we resign ourselves to thinking that only such giants can glean from Romans the full breadth and depth of its richness.

Indeed, the study of the book of Romans is not to be taken lightly (not that the study of other books can be taken lightly). Of all of the apostle Paul's letters, Romans probably presents the fullest exposition of his theology, and those who have spent many more years studying it than you and I could attest that every reading of it brings insights anew. But there are several factors that should encourage us non-giants in pressing forward with Romans.

The first is the perspicuity, or clarity, of the Scriptures, or as Luther put it, the external clearness of the Word—"all things that are in the Scriptures, are by the Word brought forth into the clearest light, and proclaimed to the whole world."[1] The *Westminster Confession of Faith* states, "All things in Scripture are not alike plain in themselves, nor alike clear unto all; yet those things which are necessary to be known, believed, and observed, for salvation, are so clearly propounded and opened in some place of Scripture or other, that not only the learned, but the unlearned, in a due use of the ordinary means, may attain unto a sufficient understanding of them."[2] Sure, we may want to place Romans in the less "plain" or less "clear" end of the spectrum, but we take heart in that the crucial message of Romans is open to sufficient understanding for all. The second is that our loving Father does not leave us to ourselves, but gives us the Spirit, who searches the depths of God, without whom Luther says no man "sees one iota in the Scriptures," but with whom Luther also says we can experience internal clearness of the Word.[3]

We are truly blessed with the perspicuity of the Scriptures and the Holy Spirit, the interpreter of spiritual truths. And fortunately for us, we have additional help in our efforts to study Romans. We have the teachings of learned men whom God has given to the church to aid it in its understanding of his glorious Word.

One such man is Dr. Paul Jeon, who offers this helpful primer on Romans. Paul is man of several academic degrees (not the least of which is a PhD in biblical studies with an emphasis on the New Testament), but at heart he is

1. Martin Luther, *The Bondage of the Will*, trans. Henry Cole (Grand Rapids: Baker, 1976), 29.

2. *Westminster Confession of Faith* 1.7.

3. Luther, *Bondage of the Will*, 29.

a pastor. His genuine concern that all believers understand the Scriptures and apply God's Word in their lives, to their blessing and benefit, can readily be seen in this book. He clearly appreciates and is humbled by the depth of what Romans has to offer, and hopes that all of us can continue to increase our grasp of its richness and dive deeper into its content. But he also recognizes the need to help organize our approach to this letter, and has provided an introduction to Romans that will prove to be an accessible door through which many of us will begin to see what the giants of the faith have reaped from the letter throughout the ages.

Paul, who is appropriately the namesake of the apostle, also shows his pastoral character by expounding not just on the meaning of the text but what the text practically means for us within the realms of church and culture (which lends this book especially well to group study). As a congregation member under Paul's shepherding, I regularly benefit from his exhortation to apply the Word in our immediate contexts, and I am positive that readers of this book will benefit likewise.

Calvin, in his dedicatory letter to Simon Grynaeus prefacing his commentary on Romans, recalled they had often discussed that "the chief excellency of an expounder consists in *lucid brevity*."[4] I contend here that Paul has given us an initiation, of lucid brevity, into Romans and the wonders of God's sovereignty and grace. I am quite certain that though it is short, and designed to rouse our interest in further study, we will find ourselves coming back to it again

4. John Calvin, *Commentary on the Epistle of Paul the Apostle to the Romans*, trans. John Owen (Grand Rapids: Eerdmans, 1947), xxiv.

and again, and gleaning from it insights anew. In that way, it thoroughly mirrors the letter on which it expounds.

Soli Deo Gloria,
Paul Jin
Church layman
February 28, 2011

Preface

IT WAS my university pastor, Duke Kwon, who first introduced me to Romans during my junior year at Brown University. Looking back now I realize how little I understood even after sitting under his thoughtful instruction. Nevertheless, this first encounter with Romans was the first major step toward understanding why Saint Paul was "not ashamed of the gospel" (1:16).

During my doctoral studies, I had the privilege of working as a research assistant for Frank Matera, an insightful scholar, clear writer, and true gentleman, who was at that time working on a Romans commentary for Baker Academic. Watching him in action and assisting him in the little ways I could was the second major step toward understanding this amazing letter. His influence on my interpretation of Romans is ineffable.

Between these two major steps I read whatever I could on Romans and wrote several unpublished papers on different sections. Throughout this time, I thought of writing a "CliffsNotes–type summary" for Romans to clarify my own thinking on the letter. But the true impetus for actually sitting down and writing a brief introductory study came after two separate attempts to teach the letter to my congregation. Despite the availability of excellent commentaries, I was unable to find a suitable resource that was fully accessible to my congregation members. Even those who understood the recommended resources found that they were too long and technical to work through from cover to cover. (This may speak more to the intended context or audience of the providers rather than the merits of the resources themselves.)

For this reason I wanted to write a brief study on the letter that introduces the novice to some of the major themes of the letter, using "R-O-M-A-N-S" itself as an acronym (see chapter 1). In addition, this brief study presents the themes by following the flow of the letter's body (1:18–15:13) with the exception of the last two studies, which invert the related sections of the letter. By doing so, I hope the reader will gain not only an appreciation of some of the more important themes of the letter but also a sense of its general flow. Thus, as the title suggests, this short work aims to serve the sole purpose of introducing a person to Romans, nothing more, nothing less. My hope is that the reader then will be encouraged to take up a more detailed exposition of the entire letter with the help of much more gifted commentators.

Meeting new people and encountering new subjects always require learning some new vocabulary. I have made every effort to avoid technical language in this study, but it is impossible to avoid altogether theological jargon in one's explanation of Romans given its rich theology (the study of God). (This inevitability is seen even in the chapter headings!) For this reason I have provided simple definitions of the theological terms that one will encounter in this study immediately after their first occurrence.

While I take full responsibility for the many shortcomings of this work, I wish to express my gratitude to several individuals. First, I thank Ms. Su Jin Kim, Mrs. Elsie Choi, and Mrs. Grace Sinn, who carefully read the manuscript several times and made valuable suggestions for improving it. I also want to thank Mr. Paul Jin and Mr. Jimmy Choi, who continue to sharpen my understanding of the apostle's gospel through regular conversations—sometimes debates—over dinner. I am also grateful to the community group leaders at CCPC Metro, whose questions and comments have often forced me to revisit the text, thereby enabling me to grow in my own understanding of this wondrous letter.

Finally, I am most grateful to my wife, whose contributions to this study and to my life are innumerable.

Paul S. Jeon
December 21, 2010

1

Introduction

BRIEF BACKGROUND COMMENTS TO ROMANS

WHY DID Paul write Romans, a letter directed to the Christians in Rome? This question is worthwhile to consider because its answers help us better understand both the message and the approach taken in the letter. Here we will consider three pieces of background information.

First, Paul, the author of the letter who introduces himself as a "slave of God, called to be an apostle [a person who is sent to represent], and set apart for the gospel of God" (1:1),[1] believed that his mission work was finished in the areas surrounding Asia Minor. He now wanted to expand his gospel ministry west of Rome to include Spain. Thus he writes in Romans 15:23–24, "But now that there are no more opportunities in these areas, and given I have wanted for many years to come to you as I journey to Spain, I hope to visit you during my journey and to be helped by you after I have first enjoyed your company for a while."

---

1. All translations represent the original translation of the author of this study.

Rome was a strategic city not only because of its nearness to Spain but also because there were already many Christians there who could provide Paul with spiritual, emotional, and material support. Securing their trust and assistance, therefore, was of great importance. This is partially why Paul goes out of his way to note his imminent trip to Jerusalem where he will deliver financial support to the Christians there on behalf of the churches in Macedonia and Achaia (15:26–27); he wanted to highlight to the Christians in Rome that he was already considered trustworthy.

Second, it appears that the believers in Rome had heard about Paul's letter to the Galatians. Paul is writing to a group of Christians that he has not met. Unlike some of his other letters to churches in cities where he had ministered prior to writing, at the time of this letter he has not founded churches in Rome. As such, Paul wants Roman Christians to know him better directly through his writing rather than through hearsay or letters addressed to other churches. In the letter to the Galatians, Paul seemed to have a very negative view toward the Mosaic Law. Indeed, without a full understanding of both the reason for the letter and the literary context of various statements, much of what Paul wrote could have been perceived as a low view of the Law. It was necessary, therefore, for Paul to write an extended statement of his gospel and to clarify in particular his understanding of the Law. This is also why Paul, in his discourse, frequently anticipates possible objections against his gospel and addresses them plainly. For instance, some believers in Rome were concerned that Paul's grace-driven gospel would lead to immoral behavior. Knowing this, Paul writes in Romans 6:1–2, "What shall we say then? Are we to continue in sin that grace may increase? Absolutely not! How can we who have died to sin still live in it?"

Third, Romans was written to address some present differences that had arisen among the Christians in Rome. Through a series of events the makeup of the church had changed significantly and had become more diverse. Formerly, the Roman churches consisted primarily of Jewish Christians. There were some gentile (non-Jewish) converts, but the churches were still mostly Jewish. But between the Jews' temporary expulsion from Rome and their return several years later, the gentiles rose to influence. It is easy to understand why tensions erupted. The apostle was confronted again with the problem of division in the local churches. Romans, therefore, can be viewed as Paul's attempt to explain how salvation through faith in Christ leads to reconciliation between all ethnicities. Using theological terms, we could say that Romans is about resolving a problem of ecclesiology (the study of church) from the perspective of soteriology (the study of salvation). For this reason, readers of Romans will encounter the repeated use of the phrase, "to the Jews first and also to the Greek" (e.g., 1:16; 2:9, 10).

SOME NOTES ON THE LETTER'S INTRODUCTION AND CONCLUSION

Given that this short study on Romans focuses on the body of the letter (1:18–15:13), it may be helpful to make some comments on the letter's introduction (1:1–17) and conclusion (15:14–16:27), which frame the body. Often readers of Romans will disregard the frame because the body contains the "meat" of Paul's gospel. The frame, however, is useful for learning about his circumstances and reasons for writing the letter. Most important, the frame helps us to read the body of the letter in light of Paul's relationship to the Roman Christians. Recognizing that his success in the west depends on their help, he carefully pens the frame to establish a sense of solidarity with the Roman Christians, as noted above.

The letter's introduction (1:1–17) has four parts: a long greeting (1:1–7), a thanksgiving prayer (1:8–10), Paul's travel plans (1:8–15), and a summary of the gospel (1:16–17) that Paul will expand on in the body of the letter. The letter's conclusion echoes some themes found in the introduction. For example Paul highlights his calling as an apostle to the gentiles (compare 1:5b and 15:18), explains why he has been unable to come to Rome (compare 1:13b and 15:22), expresses his desire to visit the Roman believers (compare 1:11a and 15:24a), and reiterates the gospel's Old Testament (OT) roots and focus on Jesus Christ (compare 1:2–3 to 15:19 and 16:26a). Like the introduction, the conclusion seeks to strengthen Paul's relationship with the Christians in Rome.

KEY THEMES

Although Romans does not contain a complete summary of Paul's core beliefs, it communicates many of Paul's convictions. Six of these are covered by the acronym "R-O-M-A-N-S": (1) the *r*evelation (revealing) of God's wrath (righteous anger) against the wickedness of humanity; (2) the *o*nly way to become righteous by trusting fully in Jesus

Christ for salvation; (3) being *m*ade alive in Christ to God versus being dead under the power of sin; (4) *a*dopted for glory; (5) pursuing a *n*ew lifestyle by offering one's life as a sacrifice, living, holy (set apart), and pleasing God; and (6) *s*alvation according to God's mercy (undeserved kindness). Aside from the last topic (6), which is based on Romans 9:1–11:36, these themes follow the letter's order. For (1) see 1:18–3:20; (2) 3:21–4:25; (3) 5:1–8:17; (4) 8:18–39; and (5) 12:1–15:13.

The following chapters will go into more detail on each of these themes. Here I will focus on the letter's main theme, which is summarized in Romans 1:16–17: "For I am not ashamed of the gospel, for it is the power of God for salvation for all who believe, to the Jew first and also to the Greek. For the righteousness of God is revealed in it from faith to faith, just as it is written, 'The righteous shall live by faith.'"

In these two verses Paul clusters key terms in Romans: "gospel," "salvation," "righteousness," and "faith." How do they relate to one another? To be "righteous" means to be perfect under God's law and will: one lives a perfect life not only by keeping the Ten Commandments but also by honoring God alone as opposed to exalting anyone or anything he created. The problem is that according to this standard "there is no one righteous, not even one" (3:10). How, then, can one be redeemed from his or her unrighteous state—where can "salvation" be found? Paul's answer is the "gospel" (good news), which he describes as "the power of God for salvation for all who believe [or have faith], to the Jew first and also to the Greek" (1:16). The key theme in

Romans, then, is how one can become "righteous"—"be saved"—through "faith" in accordance with Paul's "gospel."

THE APPROACH OF THIS STUDY

Each theological theme and corresponding section in Romans will be explored from three angles: (1) reflections on the Bible, (2) reflections on church, and (3) reflections on culture.

Reflections on the Bible

Chapters 2–7 each begin with a basic outline of the selected Bible section. The outline gives a big picture of what the section is about. The outline is followed by brief comments on the individual units, with an emphasis on key terms and the rhetorical flow of the section. Simply put, the goal of these initial reflections is to understand what Paul meant and what impact his words were intended to have on the original audience. This is important because before we can have a meaningful discussion on how to apply biblical truths to the way we approach church and evangelism, we need to first understand what Paul meant to say. I strongly recommend reading the selected verses both before and after reading through this first section. My comments will make more sense through this simple but important exercise.

Reflections on Church

A basic Christian belief is that God has not only saved individuals but that he has also formed a people for himself from every nation. As much as Western culture tends to focus on one's personal relationship with God, the Greatest Commandment—love your God and love your neighbor—reminds us that the "vertical" and the "horizontal" are tied to each other. To be a Christian, then, means to be a part of Christ's community, the church. In the second part of chapters 2–7 we will consider how we are called to live as a church community in light of the biblical reflections.

Reflections on Culture

Chapters 2–7 each conclude with some cultural reflections seeking to help Christians grow in their ability to engage their surrounding culture with the gospel in thoughtful and relevant ways. The underlying assumption here is that God's truth is relevant for all people—believers and unbelievers alike. In order to be more effective in their efforts to share the gospel, believers need to learn how to communicate biblical truths in ways that make sense and connect with unbelievers. This is not to say that we can or should "bend" biblical truths in order to make them more acceptable. However, even if unbelievers disagree with what we believe, they should never leave a conversation with the impression that Christians are unthinking and detached people. We become more credible representatives of the gospel when we train ourselves to intelligently and compassionately engage culture in light of our biblical convictions.

AN OUTLINE OF ROMANS

2

Revelation of God's Wrath

REFLECTIONS ON ROMANS 1:18—3:20

THE FIRST section of the body of Romans can be arranged in the following manner:

1:18–32:   The Unrighteousness of the Gentiles

2:1—3:8:   The Unrighteousness of the Jews

3:9–20:   The Unrighteousness of All People

The gospel is a message for both the Jew and the Greek (1:16). Unsurprisingly, Paul addresses both groups in the opening section of his presentation of his gospel. First, he addresses the gentiles (1:18–32) who have denied God's "eternal power and divine nature" (1:20), which are, according to Paul, clearly reflected in creation. Instead of giving glory to God the Creator, gentiles have surrendered their hearts in worship and service to created things and thus have become idolaters (worshipers of false gods) (1:25). Consequently, "the wrath of God is revealed from heaven" (1:18), expressed in God handing them over "to impurity, to the degradation of their bodies with one another" (1:24), "shameful passions" (1:26), and "to a warped mind to do what ought not to be done" (1:28).

Second, he addresses the Jews (2:1—3:8) who pass judgment on the gentiles, all the while expecting that they will escape God's wrath even though they are hypocrites who do the very things that they condemn (2:1-2). Possessing the Mosaic Law (the Law given through Moses) or circumcision (the external mark of God's people) does not change the fact that on "the day of wrath when God's righteous judgment is revealed, God will reward each person according to what he or she has done" (2:5-6). Hence, Paul says, "For circumcision has value *if* you keep the law, but if you break the law, your circumcision is of little worth" (2:25).

Paul's statements in 2:1-3:8 are not meant to minimize the privileges that Jews have. After all, "The Jews were entrusted with the oracles of God" (3:2). Paul's purpose, however, is to set the stage for the final unit (3:9-20) where he declares that all, both Jews and Greeks, are "under the rule of sin" (3:9). Verse 9 presents sin as a personal force that has subjected all people under its power, making them slaves to unrighteousness. Therefore, despite their best efforts, people can never obey God perfectly. Thus Paul's statement, "For by keeping the law no person will be justified [declared righteous] before God" (3:20).

Romans 1:18—3:20 is saying much more than simply, "People do bad things." Key statements in this first section (e.g., "they became ineffective in their reasoning, and their foolish hearts were darkened" [1:21]; "they exchanged the truth of God for a lie and worshiped and served the creature instead of the Creator" [1:25]; "do you look down on the riches of his kindness and tolerance and patience" [3:4];

"there is no fear of God in their eyes" [3:18]) indicate that there is something *fundamentally* wrong within all people. As theologians (people trained in theology) have said, there is something "fallen" about humanity; left to ourselves, we cannot not break from the power of sin.

REFLECTIONS ON CHURCH

Many books on "doing" church—and almost all business books—highlight that effectiveness depends on "knowing your audience." Identify what their needs, wants, and preferences are; align your goods and services; and expect success. There is practical wisdom in this advice, but Paul's teaching in the first section of the body of the letter focuses less on people's needs and wants and more on who (or what) they are. In short, he asserts that all people are under the power of sin (3:9), such that without God's supernatural intervention, they are doomed to remain slaves to futile thinking and dishonorable passions.

This message of "doom and gloom" is unpopular both inside and outside the church. Even conservative Christians overestimate people's goodness and underestimate the power and extent of sin. However, if what Paul says is true (and we believe it is), *and* if people generally turn away from this truth about humanity's fallen nature, it is even more necessary for churches to be proactive about reminding people of this truth so that the good news of salvation through faith in Jesus Christ is not lost. After all, if people do not believe in sin, they will not recognize their need for the Savior.

For this reason, it is necessary to include in every Sunday worship a section (arguably an extended section) where people are reminded of their fallen state. Songs and prayers that highlight the wide and profound power of sin and the salvation that comes through faith in Jesus Christ should be a regular part of the service.

More than a few people will be put off by this emphasis on sin. "Life is already such a downer—shouldn't church be a place where our spirits are encouraged?" Indeed, church is a place where the broken find healing, the lonely find community, and the sad find comfort. But our emphasis on sin simply reflects the Bible's own emphasis on our fallen condition, apart from which the good news about righteousness through Christ makes little sense. One could say that our intention here is not to minimize joy but rather to maximize it.

Second, this message of humanity's unrighteousness apart from Christ highlights the importance of prayer. Churches that depend solely or mainly on their planning and ability to execute simply have not taken the power and pervasiveness of sin seriously enough. Within this approach is the quiet belief that people and programs can change and ultimately save people. Paul's teaching in this section of Romans, however, stresses our fallenness—a condition so overpowering that a person cannot change and become righteous apart from God's intervention. Recognizing this, churches should conduct regular prayer meetings where their members earnestly pray that God will open blind eyes and break sin's grip on people. A church's attitude toward prayer reveals whether it truly believes Paul's message concerning the power of sin.

REFLECTIONS ON CULTURE

It is safe to assume (as noted above) that most people do not share the apostle's view of sin and humanity. The language of sin is becoming increasingly absent both within our culture and even in the pulpit. Instead, people prefer to believe that they are free to do whatever they want and that with enough education and hard work anything can be accomplished. In short, they are in control of their lives, and their sin does not control them. The idea that all people are under the power of sin is almost laughable.

The current debate on homosexuality illustrates this rejection of the idea of sin. While the debate is complex, much of it centers on issues of either personal preference or biological predisposition: either a person is free to pursue a relationship with anyone he or she pleases, or a person has no choice. Either way, sexuality is a matter of personal choice or genetic fate—it is never discussed in terms of sin.

It is important to point out that Paul (and the Bible) does *not* look at homosexuality as the "ultimate" sin. It is simply one of many ways to illustrate the result of idolatry (1:25). The main point here is that mainstream culture—including many people who claim to be Christian—has dismissed traditional and biblical notions of sin and instead understands it as bad behavior that can be corrected through discipline, education, and reinforcement; we do not need divine intervention to save us from our sins.

How should a Bible-believing Christian who believes that everyone is under the power of sin (Romans, after all, is not ambiguous about this point) engage a culture that has dismissed this view of humanity? Perhaps the best and most recent model of dialoging culture about this particular truth is Timothy Keller's *Counterfeit Gods*. While maintaining that everyone is under sin, Keller takes an indirect route of demonstrating the reality and power of idols by using contemporary examples and clear language. Specifically, he demonstrates how all people make something in creation more precious than the Creator—how all people make a good thing bad by making it an ultimate thing. He illustrates this through the common idols of love, money, success, and power, which are all good things until they become the ultimate things in our lives that then control us.[1]

DISCUSSION QUESTIONS

1. What attributes about God have you learned from this section in Romans?

2. How does the apostle define idolatry? Using Paul's definition, provide examples of contemporary, cultural, and personal idols.

3. How does Paul use the term "sin"? Is it different from your understanding of the word? If so, how?

4. Explain Paul's view of humanity's condition apart from God. How does it fit with Paul's overall gospel message?

5. How does knowing that all have sinned and fallen short of God's glory cause you to see and treat people differently?

1. Timothy Keller, *Counterfeit Gods: The Empty Promises of Money, Sex, Power, and the Only Hope That Matters* (New York: Dutton, 2009), esp. chap. 1.

6. What are some symptoms that suggest a church has lost sight of this teaching on sin and God's ensuing wrath?

7. Following the apostle Paul, Timothy Keller defines idolatry in terms of making a good thing an ultimate thing. Name several things that are inherently good but have become ultimate things in your life. How do these idols express themselves?

3

Only Way to Become Righteous

REFLECTIONS ON ROMANS 3:21—4:25

THE SECOND section of the body of Romans can be arranged in the following manner:

3:21-31   Righteousness through Faith for Jew and Gentile

4:1-25   Example: Abraham, Made Righteous through Faith

In the first section (1:18—3:20), the apostle concludes that "all, both Jews and Greeks, are under the rule of sin" (3:9). If "God will reward each person according to what he or she has done" (2:6), and if all are slaves of unrighteousness, then who can receive "eternal life" (2:7)? Who will be declared righteous before God?

In this next section, Paul declares, "But now the righteousness of God has been revealed apart from the law . . . the righteousness of God through faith in Jesus Christ for all who believe" (3:21-22). Several points are made about this "righteousness": (1) it belongs to (or comes from) God; (2) it exists "apart from the law"—apart from doing what the Mosaic Law requires; (3) it comes through "faith in Jesus Christ"; and (4) it is available to all who believe, regardless of whether they are Jews or gentiles.

In other words, on the one hand, the bad news according to Paul's gospel is that "all have sinned and fall short of the glory of God" (3:23). Left to ourselves we would be declared unrighteous and suffer the full wrath of God. On the other hand, the good news is that God has made freely available ("by his grace"; 3:24) his righteousness that is credited to a person by faith: if an individual believes that Jesus died for our unrighteousness ("he was given over for our wrongdoings"; 4:25) and was raised to life for our righteousness ("he was raised for our justification"; 4:25), then he or she will receive eternal life. This "law of faith" expresses the fact that we are justified not on the basis of our works but through faith in Jesus Christ; hence the popular Reformed phrase "justification by faith alone."

Because he knew it was a hard concept to grasp, Paul illustrates this "law of faith" through Abraham (4:1–25). Very plainly, Paul writes, "For if Abraham was declared righteous by observing the law, he had something to boast about. . . . But what does the Scripture say? 'Abraham believed in God, and it was credited to him as righteousness'" (4:2–3). Paul also notes that Abraham "received the sign of circumcision as seal of the righteousness that he had by faith while he was still uncircumcised" (4:11) to reiterate that righteousness could be credited to the uncircumcised (the gentiles) as well as the circumcised (the Jews). Therefore, Abraham is the father of all—Jew and gentile alike—who "follow in the footsteps of faith that our father Abraham had while he was still uncircumcised" (4:12). Hence, Paul can appropriately conclude this section with the declaration, "Righteousness will also be credited to us who believe in the one who raised Jesus our Lord from the dead" (4:24).

In conclusion, how does one become righteous and escape the wrath of God? Through faith alone—faith that God put forward Jesus Christ, his Son and our Lord, to atone for sins and then raised him to life for our justification (declaration of righteousness). This is the simple truth that the church has turned away from repeatedly since its beginning. Some refuse to accept this good news because they feel like "it's too easy" (referring to salvation). Something so valuable could not possibly be received for free; if it is worth having, then it must be earned with hard work. Others fear that this kind of message will result in immorality since we are saved by grace, not by works. While such distortions and misapplications of the gospel are possible, we must never compromise the truth that we become righteous by faith alone.

REFLECTIONS ON CHURCH

How should this teaching that a person becomes righteous through faith alone influence a church's "personality"? At the very least, this gospel truth should create communities characterized by humility and joy.

High and low self-esteem are really two sides of the same coin because both are based on the "law of works." A person with high self-esteem believes that he or she is performing better or meriting more than others, whether morally, financially, socially, intellectually, emotionally, or aesthetically. A person with low self-esteem believes that he or she is performing worse or meriting less than others. Both, however, assess themselves according to the "law of works," where one is owed more or less based on performance or some other related measure of worth. "Justification by faith" radically changes a person because it provides a new basis for self-evaluation. Because the person's self-worth does not rest on works but on faith in Jesus Christ, he or she suffers from neither low nor high self-esteem; his or her status depends wholly on what Christ has done. Such a person soon becomes "self-forgetful"—less concerned about what he or she and others think of his or her accomplishments—because his or her only boast is in Christ.

Similarly, a "self-forgetful" church does not take itself too seriously. It is not consumed by numbers and reputation. It does not take pride in its ministry accomplishments or in its devotion to doctrine. Rather, its only boast is in what God has done in Christ Jesus. It glories in the righteousness that God offers through faith in the crucified and risen Son.

Second, "justification by faith" provides the foundation for rejoicing always. This truth does not make us blind to the harsh realities of life; even Christians still suffer. Cancer is still cancer; loneliness is still loneliness. Still, that we are declared righteous by faith despite our sinful past helps us better understand what one Christian writer meant in his answer to the common question, "How are you doing?" "Better than I deserve."[1]

When a church understands that (1) all are under the power of sin and destined for condemnation, and (2)

---

1. C. J. Mahaney, *The Cross Centered Life: Keeping the Gospel the Main Thing* (Sisters, OR: Multnomah, 2002), 84.

righteousness is offered as a gift that is received by faith, then there is always reason to rejoice. A church rooted in justification by faith will therefore project an enduring sense of joy that will both confound and attract the watching world.

REFLECTIONS ON CULTURE

Many people today claim to believe in God. If asked whether they are religious, the answer is "no," but this answer is immediately qualified by the statement, "But I believe in God—I just don't believe in institutionalized religion."

It is helpful at this stage to probe a bit. What is this god like? Some might respond that they do not like the term "god" and prefer to use the term "force" or "higher being." Either way, what is interesting about this "god" is that it embodies what people think he/she/it should be. In this sense, this "god" is really no god but a product of the person's imagination or preference. And, more often than not, this being is all-loving, all-forgiving, and all-accepting.

In contrast, Christians believe in a God who is not only loving but also just. Paul says that "God presented Jesus as a sacrifice of atonement through faith in his blood to demonstrate his justice at the present time, because in his divine patience he had overlooked former sins" (3:25). In other words, we worship a God who takes seriously not only love but also justice. Because he is loving, he made a way to save us by presenting Jesus as a sacrifice of atonement; because he is just, he had to punish for sins. To suppose that God is nothing but all-loving is to diminish his greatness. If we do not esteem God as a being who values righteousness and justice, then the beauty of justification by faith fades quickly.

One might respond by asking why we have to be so "dogmatic" about our view of God. The gospel becomes altogether unintelligible apart from a "right" understanding of God. If, in fact, he is all-loving and ultimately does not care about our sins and will instead just gloss over them, then the statement "But now the righteousness of God has been revealed apart from the law . . . the righteousness of God through faith in Jesus Christ for all who believe" (3:21–22) is meaningless. Who cares if there is a way to become righteous through faith in Jesus if at the end of the day God does not distinguish between the righteous and the unrighteous? For this reason, an important aspect of engaging culture with the gospel is getting people to think through their beliefs about God.

DISCUSSION QUESTIONS

1. What attributes about God have you learned from this section on Romans?

2. What are four aspects of "the righteousness of God through faith in Jesus Christ"?

3. What is the good news?

4. How does Paul illustrate the "law of faith" through the life of Abraham?

5. How is salvation simultaneously free and costly?

6. How does the gospel declaration of justification by faith alone result in humility and joy?

7. How does the belief that God is nothing but all-loving diminish his character and glory?

4

Made Alive in Christ

REFLECTIONS ON ROMANS 5:1—8:17

THIS THIRD section of the body of Romans can be arranged in the following manner:

In the first section (1:18—3:20), Paul concludes that no one is righteous, neither Jew nor gentile. All are guilty of exalting something in creation over the Creator and are, consequently, guilty of idolatry. In the second section (3:21—4:25), Paul declares that a righteousness from God has now been made known and is received by faith.

Abraham not only illustrates what it means to be justified but also is the father of all who trust in Jesus for salvation, Jew and gentile alike. In this next section we consider the results of justification, namely that we are dead to sin and made alive to God in Christ (5:1—8:17).

Justification is immediate, that is, when we believe that Jesus died for our sins and was raised to life for our justification, we are declared righteous before God. Christ Jesus has atoned for our past, present, and future sins, and by faith we are credited his righteous status. Thus we are brought into a new state of righteousness.

In Romans 5:1–11 Paul invites his audience to think through some results of justification. Previously, our sins made us enemies of God, but now "we have peace with God through our Lord Jesus Christ" (5:1). Also, instead of wrath, we look forward to salvation and glory with great confidence because of God's love, which "has been poured into our hearts through the Holy Spirit" (5:5). Paul invites his audience to consider even further the greatness of God's love: "But God shows his love for us in that while we were still sinners, Christ died for us" (5:8). In other words, even when we were unrighteous and unlovable, God loved us. How much more, then, can we be confident of God's love now that we are righteous and lovable?

We have peace and joy because we now belong to a new family—more specifically, we are united to a new family head (5:12–21). This next unit reflects what theologians call "Paul's two-Adam framework." Formerly, all were condemned because Adam, humanity's representative, fell into sin. As difficult as it is for individualistic people to understand, within this framework, when Adam sinned, "death spread to all people because all sinned in Adam" (5:12). On the other hand, Jesus Christ is the "second" or "new" Adam, and he succeeded in obeying God perfectly. All who are united to him by faith "will be made righteous" (5:19). In summary, every human being, according to the apostle, belongs either to the first Adam and so dies, or to the Second Adam and so is made alive.

In Romans 6 Paul wants his audience to consider the implications of being made alive in Adam: what does it mean to be one with Christ? In the first half of the chapter, Paul addresses the question, "Are we to keep on sinning so that grace may increase?" (6:1) His emphatic answer, "Absolutely not" (6:2), makes sense within the two-Adam framework: those who are now one with Christ share in the realities and consequences of Christ's death and resurrection. In his death, believers died to sin: "We know that our old self was crucified with him so that the body of sin might be made powerless, so that we would no longer be slaves to sin. For the one who has died has been set free from sin" (6:6–7). In his resurrection, believers have been made alive to "pursue a new life" (6:4). Therefore, being united to the Second Adam, "are we to keep on sinning so that grace may increase? Absolutely not!" Rather, we should consider ourselves dead to sin and alive to God in Christ, and we should no longer present the parts of our bodies "to sin as instruments for unrighteousness but . . . to God as instruments for righteousness" (6:13). To Paul, it just does not make sense that one who is united to Christ will seek to increase sin.

In Romans 6:15–7:6, Paul addresses a similar question: "Are we to keep on sinning because we are not under law but under grace?" (6:15) Again, he responds, "Absolutely not!" (6:15) Paul notes in 3:9 that no one is really "free"; rather, all are under the power of sin. This same assumption continues in this unit and is stated plainly in 6:16: "Do you not know that if you present yourselves as obedient slaves, you are slaves of the one whom you obey, either of sin, which leads to death, or of obedience, which leads to righteousness?" Thus everyone, according to Paul, is a slave; the question is, to whom are we slaves? Therefore, when Christians keep on sinning, they are living a contradiction because although they have been set free from sin, they lives as though they were still a slave of sin (6:17–18).

According to Paul, continuing in sin is like a widow who lives as if she were still bound to her husband who has died (7:6). Because she is free from the law that bound her to her husband when he was alive, she can marry another man and not be considered an adulteress (7:3). Similarly, Christians, who have died to sin in Christ, are no longer bound to sin and the law that makes us aware of sin. We now "belong to another, to him who has been raised from the dead" (7:4). In summary, it makes no sense for believers to sin because they have died to sin and now are slaves of righteousness.

Paul's statement that Christians "have died to the law through the body of Christ" (7:4) suggests that that "the law is sin" (7:7)—that the law is inherently bad and that we have now been delivered from it through Christ. To avoid that confusion, Paul clarifies his view of the law in the next unit (7:7–13). Undeniably the law is good, for through it a person comes to know what sin is. However, although the law instructs a person on how he or she should live, it does not empower the person to do what it commands. For instance, the speed limit is "good" in the sense that it instructs a person on what the appropriate speed limit is. It does not, however, empower a person to keep it. Sin then took advantage of this weakness of the law: "Sin seized the opportunity through the commandment ["Do not covet"] and produced in me every covetous desire" (7:8). Ironically, the law, which was intended to bring us life by showing us the way to life, "proved to be death" because through it "sin came alive and I died" (7:9–10). Thus Paul concludes, "Did that which is good, then, bring death to me? Absolutely not! It was *sin*, producing death in me through what is good" (7:13). The culprit, then, is not the law but sin.

In Romans 7:14–25, Paul describes our miserable condition prior to being made alive in Christ, when we were "sold as a slave to sin" (7:14). In this condition, we noticed a strange and frustrating "law" (here Paul uses law to express "principle"): "For I desire to do what is right, but I lack ability to carry it out" (7:18). Before being made alive in Christ, individuals are under the power of sin, so much so that regardless of how much they recognize the goodness of the law and try to obey it, they fail because they lack the ability to carry out the law's demands. The concluding verse to the chapter is fitting: "What a miserable person I am! Who will deliver me from this body of death" (7:24)?

In the final unit of this section (8:1–17), Paul celebrates that God has delivered us from the body of death by making us alive in Christ. As a result, the Spirit of Christ lives in us, enabling us—in contrast to "those who are in the flesh, who cannot please God" (8:8)—to "put to death the misdeeds of the body" (8:13). Because the law could not empower us to carry out the "righteous requirement of the law," God gave his Spirit through his Son so that we would "walk not according to the flesh but according to the Spirit" (8:4). This reference to the Spirit reminds the audience of the opening unit of this section where Paul says that "hope does not fail us, because God's love has been poured into our hearts through the Holy Spirit" (5:5). Romans 5:1–11 and 8:1–17, therefore, serve as bookends to this section.

REFLECTIONS ON CHURCH

At some point in your church experience, you must have heard about Adam and Eve—how God created Adam from the dust, how he created Eve from Adam, and how they fell from grace by eating the forbidden fruit. Also, you probably have some sense that things are the way they are—that is, we are no longer in paradise—because of their sin. What is perhaps missing is an appreciation of our connection to Adam: what effect did his sin have for us apart from being cast out of the Eden?

The bottom line, according to Romans 5:11–21, is that the penalty of *one* man's sin is *universal*: "Therefore, as sin came into the world through one man, and death through sin, so death spread to all men because all sinned" (5:12). In other words, the consequence of one man's sin is shared by all whom he represents, whether or not those represented selected him as their representative. Logically, then, all who are separated from Christ and therefore united to Adam are sinners—regardless of how kind and good they may appear—and will suffer the penalty of death on account of Adam's sin. For a church to accept this uncomfortable truth requires acknowledging the Bible as God's authoritative Word and recognizing the application of this commitment even if the truth seems unfair or narrow-minded.

At the same time, when we believe Paul's teaching in Romans about the significance of our union with Adam, we understand the importance of his repeated use of phrases like "*in* Christ," "*in* him," "*through* him," and so forth. Salvation comes from being united to Christ—becoming one with him—through faith. Through this union believers share in his victory: "Therefore, as one act of disobedience led to condemnation for all people, so one act of righteousness leads to justification and life for all people" (5:18). Therefore, the basic call of the gospel is *not* to good works but to faith in Christ, so that a person may no longer be united to the First Adam but to the Second, who is Jesus Christ.

Part of the concern with this teaching is that salvation seems so easy and that it encourages sinful behavior. If all it takes to become saved is faith in Jesus and if we are then counted righteous, what does it matter how we live—why not sin? This, as I noted above, is not a new question. In this section Paul addresses the question from the two-Adam framework. Specifically, in Romans 6:5–11 he says,

> If we have been united with him in his death, we will certainly be united with him in his resurrection. We know that our old self was crucified with him so that the body of sin might be made powerless, so that we would no longer be slaves to sin. For the one who has died has been set free from sin. Now if we have died with Christ, we believe that we will also live with him. We know that since Christ has been raised from the dead,

> he will never die again; death no longer has mastery over him. For the death, he died he died to sin once for all; but the life he lives he lives to God. *So you also* must consider yourselves dead to sin and alive to God in Christ Jesus.

A true Christian, therefore, cannot keep on sinning "so that grace may increase" (6:1) or "because we are not under the law but under grace" (6:14). Believing in Jesus Christ means believing that one has died with Christ in his death on the cross and that one will share in his resurrection; therefore, one must consider oneself dead to sin and alive to God through Christ. In short, a sinful life is a paradox for a true believer.

There are at least two applications for churches to consider. First, while a gospel-centered church should frequently and passionately preach and teach that a person is saved by faith alone, it should also emphasize with just as much frequency and passion why a sinful life is unacceptable. When a person persists in sin, such a church should practice church discipline, exhorting the individual to recognize how their life contradicts the significance of being united to Christ. In other words, a gospel-centered church should never become complacent with sin but should be committed to developing holiness among its members.

Second, a gospel-centered church should regularly encourage its members to carefully consider whether their faith is genuine. The clear implication from this section is that if a person keeps on sinning—if he or she "presents the parts of his or her body as slaves to impurity and lawlessness" (6:19), he or she may not suffer from a lack of understanding the gospel; rather, he or she may not, in fact, be united to Christ. We hesitate to challenge one another in this regard lest others think that we are being judgmental and ungracious. It is true that God alone knows the hearts of people and who is truly saved. Still, part of the reason Paul devotes so much space to discussing the matter of being made alive in Christ is to help us discern for ourselves—and for others—whether our faith is genuine.

REFLECTIONS ON CULTURE

Perhaps the best way to communicate Paul's two-Adam christology to non-Christians is through sports. As much as contemporary people want to see themselves as individuals, their loyalties to their sports team betray a deep desire to connect to someone or something bigger than themselves. Hence, when "my Redskins" win, *we* win (even though I had nothing to do with their winning).

Another analogy is our curious devotion to Hollywood figures and television shows. Why the obsession to keep up with certain stars? Why the excitement when a person's favorite show is about to begin a new season, and why the depression when that show comes to an end? Romans invites us not only to admit that we make such connections with certain teams, people, and shows, but also to consider *why*.

An objection commonly raised to Paul's two-Adam framework relates to whether Adam was an actual person or a mythical character. Sometimes the historicity of Adam seems even less credible than the virgin birth. "Really—Adam came from the dust, and then God breathed new life into him? Doesn't that sound a bit odd—a bit mythical?" Therefore, getting to the point of even considering how

Adam's individual sin had universal effects is difficult when a person does not even believe that he was an actual person.

At this point, it may be helpful to ask, "How, then, do you explain the widespread nature of immorality across time and culture?" The Bible's answer is that everyone became a sinner when Adam, humanity's representative, sinned. The unbeliever may respond, "You believe that because you have faith in the Bible. But scientific research suggests that people are immoral because . . ." Important to notice here is that even the unbeliever has a sacred text, whether that text is the writings of Charles Darwin or Stephen Hawking. The point is that both people have faith in their own sacred texts. Recognizing this reality will help the discussion progress from statements like, "Some people have faith and some don't" to thoughtful discussions of people's worldviews (people's perspectives of the world) and conversations on which worldview provides a better account for reality.

DISCUSSION QUESTIONS

1. What attributes about God have you learned from this section on Romans?

2. List and explain some results of justification.

3. Explain the meaning and significance of "Paul's two-Adam framework." What are some ways to communicate Paul's two-Adam christology? Come up with one or two illustrations.

4. Are we to sin more so that grace may increase? How does the apostle answer this question?

5. Are we to sin more because we are not under law but under grace? How does the apostle answer this question?

6. Does Paul believe that "the law is sin"?

7. What does the Spirit accomplish which the law could not? How does one receive the Spirit?

8. What role does Paul's emphasis on our union with Christ play in his discussion on questions pertaining to sin? In other words, why should we not sin as a result of our union with Christ?

5

Adopted for Glory

THIS FOURTH section of the body of Romans can be arranged in the following manner:

> 8:18–27:   Future Glory
>
> 8:28–39:   Confidence amidst Suffering

The first unit can be divided further along the headings "Future Glory" (8:18–24a) and "Hope through
Perseverance and the Spirit" (8:24b–27). In the first subunit,
Paul affirms that the glory that will be revealed when Christ
returns will be so glorious that even the immense suffer-
ings of the present pale in comparison (8:18). Christians,
who have already received the gift of the Spirit as a down
payment, will experience the "redemption of their bodies"
(8:23) at this time. There will be no more disease, decay, and
demise. From this perspective, it can be said that the proper
Christina disposition is anticipation of glorification. Then,
going somewhat on a tangent, he speaks of this day from
the perspective of the rest of creation (8:19–22). When "the
children of God are revealed" (8:19), creation itself will

be freed from its enslavement to deterioration and death. Personifying creation, Paul compares its longing for freedom to a pregnant woman who awaits the birth of her child.

In Romans 8:24b–27 Paul adds two comments about how we are to hope as we wait for our glorification. First, he makes the obvious point that hope that is "seen" (realized) can no longer be hoped for (8:24b). Therefore, learning to persevere is an important Christian discipline. We are, however, not left to do our best on our own. Paul reminds believers that they have the Spirit who prays for them especially during their times of weakness (8:26). And we are confident that God hears these requests because the Spirit prays according to God's will (8:27).

The second unit can also be divided along the two themes "What Christians Know" (8:28–30) and "What Christians Conclude" (8:31–39). First, believers know that they have been predestined, called, justified, and glorified (8:30). They have been predestined (chosen) to be transformed into the likeness of Jesus Christ; they have been called according to God's plan of redemption; they have been justified through faith in Christ; and they will also be glorified (exalted) when Christ returns.

Knowing this, they can conclude with the apostle Paul, "We are more than conquerors through him who loved us" (8:37). In Romans 8:31–35 Paul lays out a series of rhetorical questions: "If God is for us, who can be against us?" "Will he not graciously give us all things, given that he has given us his son?" "Who will bring any charge against God's chosen ones?" "Who will condemn those for whom Christ died?" These questions set the stage for the glorious conclusion that nothing—absolutely nothing—can separate us from the love of God that is in Christ Jesus.

In conclusion, Christians are to remain hopeful and confident in the face of suffering. Their hope lies in the promise that all of creation will be redeemed and will share in Christ's glory when he returns. Therefore, they ought to persevere with patience and through the help of the Spirit. Their confidence lies in God's sovereign love that has predestined, called, justified, and glorified them. They ought to conclude with the apostle that "neither death nor life, neither angels nor demons, neither the present nor the future, nor any powers, neither height nor depth, nor anything else in all creation, will be able to separate us from the love of God that is in Christ Jesus our Lord" (8:38–39).

REFLECTIONS ON CHURCH

The church should be marked with hope. First, the church should be hopeful through suffering, which the Bible makes clear is inevitable for believers. How anyone can believe that following Christ Jesus will guarantee a life of prosperity and health is a mystery. Unfortunately, this is a view that is seemingly increasing in popularity within the church. Jesus himself said, "Take up your cross and follow me" (Matt. 16:24). It is more appropriate to assume that following Jesus will result in a life of suffering. At the same time, Romans 8:18–39 reminds Christians to remain joyful and confident in the face of suffering because of the hope we have in Christ.

Second, the church should be hopeful for creation. Many Christians have a "Platonic" view of the world. They believe that the body is bad and the soul good; the material evil and the immaterial admirable. Salvation, therefore, is understood as freedom from this body and world; we will be whisked away to heaven. This view of salvation basically believes that God has abandoned his original creation and will take the elect to another world of bliss and life. If this is the case, why should Christians care about this world? After all, if God himself has given up on the world and plans on starting over elsewhere, why not let it rot away?

We care about creation because God cares about creation. Romans 8:18–24a reminds us that the message of salvation is one of *cosmic* redemption: God cares for everything he created, which was initially good but is now fallen. He cares about pollution, animal abuse, disease, cancer, infertility, and so forth. Christ's resurrection signals a new era of life not only for believers but also for all of creation. A Christian, therefore, cannot be indifferent to the fallen condition of the present world.

Because Jesus Christ has not yet returned, suffering, disease, and death continue. Indeed, Christ has won the war, but the battle with sin and its effects continues. Believers, however, have already received the gift of the Spirit. The Spirit is a deposit—a hint, foreshadow, guarantee—of the final and full redemption that will take place when Christ returns. Through the help of the Spirit believers must learn the discipline of persevering in hope as they anticipate the Day of Glory.

Given their hope of glory, Christians are uniquely able to address suffering and the fallen state of this world. The contemporary hymn "All Must Be Well" expresses the believer's conviction, which is based on the closing verses of

Romans 8. Because nothing can separate us from the love of God, all will be well. In this sense a church should be a place where it is easy to speak about and be honest regarding suffering, because the discussion and experience of suffering will always conclude on a note of hope and confidence.

REFLECTIONS ON CULTURE

I recently asked a friend (let us call him "Max") who is not a Christian what his view of the future is. Concerning his personal future, he said that he hoped to succeed in establishing his own company and retire early in order to travel, eat, drink, and be merry. Concerning the future of the world, he said that he would not be surprised if there were flying cars and regular trips to and from the moon. Concerning the environment, he said that he was relatively indifferent so long as it lasted long enough for him and his children. At the end of our conversation, he said that perhaps technology would become so advanced that it would solve all the problems related to world hunger and pollution.

When I asked him, "Don't you feel that 'things are not the way they're supposed to be'—that cancer is 'wrong,' as well as child abuse, genocide, and so on?" he responded, "All that is just a part of life—you can't save the world, let alone your soul." When most people look at Max, they see a person who does not have a care in the world and is a respectable, diligent, and happy-go-lucky fellow. When I see him, I see a person who is without hope that there will be a "better" future—a redeemed future.

There are many people who have succeeded in creating their heaven on earth and therefore do not long for cosmic redemption. On the whole, their lives are marked by tremendous material success, and as time passes they become more thankful that they have been able to live the "good life." While recognizing that others do not share in their good fortune, they are not disturbed very much by their unfortunate lot.

Communicating the hope of glory to such people is difficult. After all, regardless of how eloquent and knowledgeable Christians are, they will not be very effective with a person who is indifferent to cosmic redemption and future glory. What *will* gain their attention and respect, however, is the believer's good works and uncommon perspective on life. When Christians live humbly and sacrificially, they make non-Christians curious. Why would this missionary with an established career choose to give up everything to go to this poor country where he is unable to speak the language and where there are no comforts of developed countries? Why is she hopeful and joyful in the face of cancer? These "strange" and "troubling" decisions and responses plant the seeds of interest in the hearts and minds of unbelievers. "I want what they have—I want that kind of hope, strength, and confidence." In short, when Christians live according to a new hope, fully confident that they have been predestined, called, justified, and glorified; when they believe fully that nothing can separate them from the love of God, those around them become curious about their hope. And that is when the dialogue begins.

DISCUSSION QUESTIONS

1. What attributes about God have you learned from this section on Romans?

2. What is the hope of glory both for the Christian and for creation? What does the day of redemption entail? How does this comfort and encourage you now?

3. How does the Spirit help believers as they await future glory? How does this comfort and encourage you now?

4. Outline the process through which Paul arrives at the conclusion, "No one and nothing in all creation can separate us from the love of God that is in Christ Jesus." What difference does this conclusion make on the thing that you are currently most concerned about or afraid of?

5. Why should Christians care about the present world? How are Christians uniquely equipped to address suffering in the present world?

6. Describe the role that our lifestyle plays in communicating the hope of glory.

6

New Lifestyle

THIS FIFTH section of the body of Romans can be arranged in the following manner:

12:1—13:14: Love and Obedience in the New Age

14:1—15:13: Welcoming One Another according to the Example of Christ

In this section, Paul presents an extensive moral exhortation in which he calls Christians to a new lifestyle in view of Christ's death and resurrection (which he has detailed in prior sections of the letter). This exhortation emphasizes the importance—arguably the necessity—of good works within Paul's gospel. The section has two parts, the first (12:1—13:14) focusing on how Christians are to live as one body in Christ through love and forgiveness, and the second (14:1—15:13) focusing on specific problems between the "strong" and "weak" believers in Rome.

The first unit has five smaller parts. The first (12:1–2) begins a new section in the letter, focusing on the new lifestyle that believers are to adopt "in view of God's mercies" (12:1). This prepositional phrase is crucial because it highlights an important relationship in Pauline thought. The "indicative-imperative relationship" basically means that given what God has done (the indicative), this is how we are to live (the imperative). This new lifestyle includes actually living for God (versus merely claiming to believe in God) and being "transformed by the renewal of your mind" (12:2). The apostle's emphasis is clear: God's saving righteousness should result in a new life of obedience—not to earn God's favor, but as an expression of gratitude for the mercies we have already received. The final clause of Romans 12:2 suggests that we can "determine the will of God" only by living differently from our previous life and from the patterns of the world.

In the second part of the first unit (12:3–8), the apostle notes an important epiphany of the renewed mind—the recognition that "although we are many, we are one body in Christ and members of one another" (12:5). In other words, a mind that has been sobered by the gospel abandons vain notions of rugged individualism. Paul's exhortation is for believers to anchor any search for purpose in the conviction that every believer has received gifts "according to the measure of faith that God has given" (12:3) for the mutual encouragement of all the saints (Christians/believers). The list that follows in 12:6–8 is not meant to be exhaustive but illustrative of different spiritual gifts.

The third part (12:9–21) contains a set of commands concerning how members are to treat one another. Romans 12:9–13 focuses on the theme of love; Romans 12:14–21 focuses on the theme of forgiveness. Keeping in mind Paul's indicative-imperative relationship, we see how the commands to love and forgive point back to how God has first loved and forgiven us in Christ Jesus. It is the duty of believers to demonstrate their experience of God's mercies by extending the same kind of love and forgiveness to one another.

The fourth part (13:1–7) is a tangent, given that Paul returns to the theme of love in the fifth part. But it does continue the theme that believers must learn to live not as individuals but as members of communities. In this fourth part, Paul instructs believers to respect "governing authorities" because "there are no authorities except from God" (13:1), which are established to "carry out God's punishment on wrongdoers" (13:4). Similarly, Paul instructs believers to pay taxes because "these authorities are God's servants who devote themselves to governing" (13:6).

The fifth and final part of the first half of this section (13:8–14) returns to the love command. Paul says that the last five commandments of the Decalogue (the Ten Commandments) are different expressions of the single command, "Love your neighbor as yourself" (13:9). To motivate Christians to love and good works, Paul reminds them that the Day of Christ is closing in: "The night is gone, the day is near. Therefore, let us put aside the deeds of darkness and put on the weapons of light" (13:12); let us love one another.

The second unit has four parts, each beginning with an exhortation. The first part (14:1–12) clues us into a significant problem in Rome. Among the Roman believers there was a division between those who were considered "weak in faith" and those who were "strong in faith." The latter believed that they could eat anything, and the former only vegetables (14:2). Paul's exhortation was for neither to judge the other, since "each person will give an account to God" (14:12), not to fellow believers.

In passing, it is important to note that Paul is *not* saying that accountability between believers is unnecessary. Many Christians have taken this passage to mean that we should never call believers to obedience and holiness. Here Paul is addressing "secondary topics" (e.g., food, observance of certain days), not central issues (e.g., how one is saved, sexual purity). Paul's concern is that believers are becoming divided over unimportant issues. The exhortation not to pass judgment is a command not to alienate themselves from one another over such petty issues.

The second part (14:13–23) is directed to those who are strong in the faith, instructing them "not to put a stumbling block or obstacle in the way of a fellow believer" (14:13). While Paul himself believes that "nothing is inherently unclean" (14:14a), he considers it appropriate to refrain from eating meat or drinking wine when necessary for the sake of "the one who thinks it is unclean" (14:14b). Similarly, those who are strong in the faith should "pursue what results in peace and mutual encouragement" (14:19) because they know that "the kingdom of God is not about eating and drinking but about righteousness and peace and joy in the Holy Spirit" (14:17). Therefore, if eating meat or drinking causes the weak believer to stumble, the strong believer should refrain from those things for the sake of unity.

In the third part (15:1–6), Paul exhorts the strong "to put up with the shortcomings of the weak" by shifting their focus away from pleasing themselves to encouraging fellow believers (15:1). Paul grounds this exhortation in the example of Christ, who lived not to please himself but to serve others (15:3). Knowing that human effort and resolve are insufficient, he prays that "the God of endurance and encouragement" would empower all the believers in Rome to live in peace—that "with one heart and voice they would glorify the God and Father of our Lord Jesus Christ" (15:5–6).

The final part (15:7–12) exhorts all the believers to welcome one another. Again Paul grounds this exhortation in Christ: "Welcome one another *as* Christ welcomed you" (15:7). Quoting from the Old Testament, Paul reiterates that Jews and gentiles have become one people through Christ (no small point given the tensions among the Roman Christians). He concludes this passage with a blessing, highlighting the repeated themes of joy, peace, and the role of the Holy Spirit in the life of the believer.

REFLECTIONS ON CHURCH

This section is full of many practical applications for the church. Here we will consider just three.

The first application is for believers to remind one another that good works matter. Paul has highlighted that we are saved by faith alone. Nevertheless, saving faith is always accompanied by a new lifestyle. Paul's emphasis that we are saved by faith—not works—should never make us less intentional about how we live. This section makes clear that we have been saved by faith unto good works. Thus, we must assert again and again that adopting a new lifestyle is important because it evidences true faith and pleases God.

Second, Paul's focus on the believer's communal responsibilities is unsettling for the contemporary believer who emphasizes "my personal relationship with God." Both units are concerned with how believers treat one another. Paul's basic exhortation regarding the new lifestyle is that believers are to be faithful church members, whether that means using one's God-given gifts for building up the body of Christ, loving much and forgiving quickly, or welcoming one another and making every effort to further peace. Being an active part of the community is not an option for believers. As I stated before, a mind that has been sobered by the gospel abandons vain notions of rugged individualism. Offering one's life to God and being transformed in one's thinking means taking church membership seriously.

Third, although the church has one basic confession—that saving righteousness comes through faith in Christ Jesus—differences will persist and sometimes multiply. Differences are inevitable because they are part of different believers' abilities to contribute to the body of Christ in unique ways, and because believers are at different levels of maturity. Differences are also inevitable because God has called people from every tribe, tongue, and nation. Knowing this, Paul exhorts believers not to allow petty divisions to break their unity in Christ but instead to love and forgive one another regularly and quickly. When believers do so, they themselves are a witness to the reconciling power of the gospel.

REFLECTIONS ON CULTURE

As noted in the last chapter, we need to see the important role that our lifestyle plays in sharing the gospel effectively. If there is nothing different about the way we live and think; if we value and pursue everything the world values and pursues; if we only love those who love us and hold a grudge against fellow believers; and if we only associate with those who come from a similar socio-economic or ethnic group, it should not surprise us that non-Christians do not think that it makes a real difference whether or not a person believes in Christ. Our claim to trust in Jesus for salvation loses credibility if, at the end of the day, we offer our lives to the gods of this world and conform to the thinking and living patterns of our culture. For these reasons, we must make every effort to live out the gospel by adopting a new lifestyle.

Specifically, believers should focus on how they treat other believers. When non-Christians sees Christians ridicule, despise, ignore, and slander one another, why would they want to join a church? How could an unbeliever come to understand Christ's unconditional love and reconciling work when there is nothing but division and hatred between believers? On the other hand, imagine the quality of our witness if we looked beyond our own comforts, needs, and preferences to those of fellow believers, or if we loved one another the way Christ loved us by forgiving one another and setting aside petty differences? Perhaps the world would begin to say, "See how they love one another," and perhaps some would even be enticed to join churches where diverse people see and treat one another as family because of Christ.

DISCUSSION QUESTIONS

1. What attributes about God have you learned from this section on Romans?

2. Explain what is meant by the "indicative-imperative relationship."

3. How do we reconcile Paul's teaching that we are saved by faith alone with his emphasis on the "necessity" of good works?

4. How does the gospel result in a renewed appreciation for community?

5. In view of God's mercies in Christ Jesus, what qualities should Christian communities exude? In what ways can you express these qualities in your church?

6. What is Paul's exhortation to those who are "strong in faith"? To those who are "weak in faith"? To both? How are these exhortations applicable today?

7. What role do our lifestyles play in communicating the gospel to our surrounding culture?

7

Salvation according to God's Mercy

REFLECTIONS ON ROMANS 9:1—11:36

T HIS SIXTH section of the body of Romans can be arranged in the following manner:

9:1–29:   Divine Election

9:30—10:21:   Israel's Failure

11:1–36:   God's Unchangeable Call

The first unit of this final section has four parts. The first (9:1–5) expresses Paul's great sorrow for his fellow Jews who have received special blessings but have ultimately rejected God's saving righteousness in Christ. Paul's expression, "I have great sorrow and continuing anguish in my heart" (9:2), is not an exaggeration. He is heartbroken because he knows that the Israelites are a special people: "To them belong the adoption, the glory, the covenants, the law, the worship, and the promises" (9:4). That the chosen people are currently "cut off from Christ" (9:2) causes distress for the apostle.

The second part (9:6–13) addresses the question of whether God has rejected historical Israel, given that there is now no distinction between Jew and gentile. Has ethnic Israel been replaced by a "new Israel," the church? In short, have God's promises to Israel failed? Paul insists that this is not the case and explains his answer through the principle of election. Contrasting the offspring of Isaac with the offspring of Ishmael, and contrasting Jacob with Esau, Paul teaches that "it is not the children of the flesh [historical-ethnic Israel] who are the children of God [true Israel], but the children of the promise" (9:8). (Note that "promise" characterized the lives and destinies of Isaac and Jacob in contrast to Ishmael and Esau.) In other words, God's Word has not failed if one understands that "true Israel" was never intended to be historical-ethnic Israel but those who are chosen and saved from Jews and gentiles according to God's mercy.

The third part (9:14–18) addresses the expected objection to the principle of election: "Is God unjust?" (9:14) Paul answers this objection by quoting from the Old Testament: "I will have mercy on whom I have mercy, and I will have compassion on whom I have compassion" (9:15; see also Exod. 33:19). By definition, mercy is not mandatory: I am not unjust because I tell one debtor to "forget about it" while forcing another debtor to pay what he or she owes. "I will have mercy on whom I have mercy." To accuse God of being unjust because he shows mercy to some is to assume that if God chooses to forgive and save some, he is obligated to forgive and save all. This obligation is man-made (and man-centered); the apostle finds no place for it.

Paul concludes this first unit (9:19–29) by addressing an objection to his response: "You will then say to me, 'Why does he still blame me? For who can resist his divine will?'"

(9:19) Paul does not directly address this objection. Instead, his answer is, "But who are you, as a human being, to talk back to God?'" (9:20) In other words, Paul is saying, "God is God, and we are not; therefore, we are in no position to challenge God and accuse him of being unjust." Using the analogy of the potter, Paul says, "Doesn't the potter have the right over the clay to make out of the same lump one thing for honorable use and another for dishonorable use?" (9:21) While Paul's response has never been popular, it reminds Christians, then and now, of the Creator-creature distinction. Just as a work of literature cannot command the author to write it a certain way, so too creation cannot tell the Creator what he can and cannot do.

The second unit (9:30–10:21) has three parts. The first (9:30–10:4) comments on the irony of Israel's situation. By trying to keep the law, Israel failed to attain the status of righteousness; the gentiles, however, have attained it without effort (9:30–31). The Israelites' failure is due to their trying to become righteousness by their own works rather than by faith (9:32). Paul does not deny their earnestness; their problem is that "they are zealous for God—but not according to knowledge" (10:2); they are "ignorant of the righteousness that comes from God and thus seek to establish their own righteousness instead of submitting to God's righteousness" (10:3).

In the second part (10:5–13), Paul reiterates that saving righteousness comes exclusively by faith, to Jew and gentile alike: "Everyone who calls on the name of the Lord will be saved" (10:13; see also Joel 2:32). Specifically, "If you confess with your mouth that Jesus is Lord and believe in your heart that God raised him from the dead, you will be saved. For with the heart one believes and is justified, and with the mouth one confesses and is saved" (10:9–10). In contrast to the righteousness that comes from obeying the law, saving righteousness is based on faith alone.

The third part (10:14–21) describes Israel's disobedience as a result of their failure to believe Paul's gospel. First, Paul establishes the principle that "faith comes from hearing, and hearing through the word of Christ" (10:17). Second, he asks, "Has Israel not heard?" and answers, "Of course Israel has heard" (10:18). Finally, he asks, "Did Israel not understand?" (10:19) He responds by quoting from Moses and Isaiah, concluding that God has offered Israel saving righteousness but that Israel has refused to submit to God's righteousness. Instead, Israel has sought a righteousness by works (10:3).

The last unit (11:1–36) has five parts. The first (11:1–6) raises and answers again the central question of this entire section: "Has God rejected his people?" (11:1) Using himself as an example ("I myself am an Israelite"; 11:1) and appealing again to the Old Testament, Paul responds, "Absolutely not!" (11:1) Rather, as in the days of Elijah, God has preserved for himself "a remnant chosen by grace" (11:5). Therefore, although all historical-ethnic Israel will not be saved, all "true Israel"—the children of promise, a remnant consisting of Jews and gentiles—will be saved.

In the second part (11:7–12) Paul compares the chosen Israelites with "the rest" of Israel: "The elect obtained it, but the rest were hardened" (11:7). After quoting several Old Testament texts, Paul then asks, "Now if the trespass of 'the rest' resulted in riches for the world, and if their failure resulted in riches for the gentiles, how much more riches will their *full number* mean?" (I italicize "full number" because I will refer to it below.) For some this question seems to suggest that "the rest" of Israel, that is, all historical-ethnic Israel, will ultimately be saved. We need to look at what Paul says in the next two parts of this unit to determine whether this is the case.

The third part (11:13–24) contains a warning to gentile Christians who were tempted to believe that they were now superior to the Jews: "Do not be arrogant toward the branches [historical-ethnic Israel] that have been broken off" (11:18). Instead, they are to remember that "the branches were broken off because of unbelief" (11:20) and to "be afraid. For if God did not spare the natural branches, he will not spare you either" (11:20–21). Paul adds that it is within God's power for the broken branches to be re-grafted if they do not continue in unbelief (11:23). The question remains, however, whether "broken branches" is referring to all historical-ethnic Israel.

The fourth part (11:25–32) indicates that "all Israel will be saved" (11:26). At first glance, it appears that Paul is saying that in the end all historical-ethnic Israel will be saved. A closer reading, however, shows that he is referring to their "full number" (11:12), which corresponds to the "full number" of gentiles who will come in (11:25). Paul asserts that an additional—and possibly large—number of ethnic Israel will be saved after the selected number of gentiles has been incorporated into "true Israel." After this period of blessing on the gentiles, God will *then* have mercy on a "full number" of Jews who are part of this post-gentile–blessing period.

In summary, Paul is not saying that all historical-ethnic Israel will be saved, for that would be an obvious contradiction to what he says about "true Israel" in Romans 9. Instead, Paul is highlighting the design of God's plan of salvation and the principle of election: when Jews expected to enjoy favor, the gentiles received salvation; and when gentiles begin to feel superior, the Jews will once again enjoy favor. Thus, grace oscillates between the Jews and gentiles according to God's mercy, not according to any rules or expectations of humanity. This design highlights God's mercy as it is revealed in election and gives him all the glory for salvation.

In the final analysis, then, God has not abandoned Israel. The flood of blessings to the gentiles, resulting in many gentile Christians, will once again flow to the Israelites, resulting in the salvation of many Jews. The gentiles have not replaced the Jews, nor has the church replaced Israel; rather, the gentiles have been incorporated into true Israel and, with the chosen Israelites—the remnant—form the people of God.

The fifth part concludes this long section with a song of adoration in response to God's wisdom, knowledge, and power (11:33–36). The context suggests that Paul is praising God specifically for his wondrous plan of salvation, which includes Jews and gentiles, both chosen according to his mercy. By concluding this extensive theological section with song, Paul reminds us that all theology should lead to doxology (praise and worship).

REFLECTIONS ON CHURCH

Our main reflection concerns the principle of election as it pertains to God's plan of salvation. In the past, biblical scholars saw Romans 9–11 as a key source for the doctrine of predestination (election). More recently, they have focused less on the doctrine of predestination and more on how the section helps us understand the relationship between Israel's destiny and God's faithfulness to his promises.

Regardless of which side one takes, this section of Romans will continue to play an important role in discussions on predestination—the belief that God has predestined some for salvation—that is, the "elect." To suppose that election has little to do with this section is just silly.

In our personal reflections and discussions on such a controversial topic, we benefit from asking ourselves, "Is my main concern for truth or for what seems fair to me?" Regardless of some of the interpretive challenges of Romans 9–11, it is clear that Paul emphasizes God's right to have mercy on whom he will have mercy and to harden whom he will harden, without taking into consideration human effort and achievement. In a word, Paul highlights that salvation depends solely on God's sovereignty and grace.

We cannot deny the consequences of what Paul says in this section, especially in 9:20–23—that God has predestined some for glory and salvation and others for wrath and condemnation. Some—most notably Karl Barth in *The Epistle to the Romans*—have argued that Augustine, Calvin, and other Reformers misrepresented Paul's doctrine of predestination through a cause-and-effect scheme. Barth believed that the more appropriate way to interpret predestination is to understand it as a way of speaking about God's "otherness"—his transcendent love and wisdom that cannot be explained and understood in time and space.[1]

In my opinion, such a reading moves away from the plain meaning of the text and is perhaps triggered rather by modern sensibilities of fair play. People want to believe that their decisions and actions play a decisive—if not ultimate—role in determining their eternal destiny. The problem, however, with moving away from this traditional understanding of election is that God is no longer sovereign *and* his grace is unnecessary; this awakens a whole new set of horrors. Imagine a world where God is not sovereign but dependent on human action. Imagine a life where our destiny rests ultimately on us rather than on grace. Based on the reality of our slavery to sin, do we really want a world where salvation is up to us? Has your experience of obedience been one of perfection? While Paul's teaching on salvation raises difficult philosophical and personal questions, it also humbles us and leaves us in wonder and awe of God's mercies.

REFLECTIONS ON CULTURE

We benefit from Paul's model of compassion for the lost and commitment to truth. Notice the stark contrast between many contemporary Christians who parade that "Gays are terrible" versus Paul's compassion for those who are cut off from Christ. Paul says, "I have great sorrow and continuing anguish in my heart. For I could wish that I

1. Karl Barth, *The Epistle to the Romans*, trans. Edwyn C. Hoskyns, 6th ed. (Oxford: Oxford University Press, 1968), 275.

myself were accursed and cut off from Christ for the sake of my brothers" (9:1–3). That we are saved by grace should never result in feelings of superiority toward others but rather compassion. Because saving righteousness does not depend on our works but rather on faith in the perfect work of Jesus Christ, there is no place for pride. We were no better than those who are currently cut off from Christ.

At the same time, it is important to observe that Paul does not shy away from the truth. He recognizes that the sincerity of "the rest" of the Jews is admirable, but then he makes clear that sincerity is not enough; rather, zeal must be rooted in knowledge. Despite his compassion for his fellow Jews, he maintains that even when people try to establish their own righteousness through a sincere and perhaps even admirable devotion to religion, saving righteousness comes from God alone, through faith alone. Often Christians have turned away from the truth because they meet "nice" people and wonder how God could really condemn such a person while Christians are living much worse lives. It can be tempting to begin entertaining the belief that perhaps good works play some role—even if a minimal role—in salvation. Nevertheless, like Paul, we must stay firm to the gospel truth that saving righteousness is purely according to God's mercy.

The other application for believers is to renew the importance of the Bible in modern and postmodern thought. In the apostle's attempt to address the thorny question of whether God has abandoned Israel, we notice his repeated use of Scripture to retell Israel's story. Similarly, the church's mission is to reestablish the authority of God's Word. Believers and unbelievers alike tend to place a higher premium on their own experiences or science or even Oprah. Working for God's glory includes redeeming the authoritative role that Scripture must have in people's lives.

DISCUSSION QUESTIONS

1. What attributes about God have you learned from this section on Romans?

2. According to the apostle, who is "true Israel"?

3. Explain what is meant by God's mercy. Do we deserve it? Does anyone?

4. What role does God's mercy play in his plan of salvation?

5. How does Paul respond to the questions, "Is God unjust?" and "Why does he still blame me?" What do your responses to Paul's responses reveal about your beliefs about God, salvation, and mercy?

6. Why is sincerity and zeal not enough for salvation? What else is needed?

7. Why is the doctrine of election such a controversial topic? What are some difficulties with accepting the apostle's teaching that we are saved according to mercy? What are some difficulties with rejecting it?

8. How does Paul exhibit both compassion and commitment to truth in his ministry? How should this instruct us as we seek to engage our surrounding culture?

8

Conclusion

THE PURPOSE of this brief study has been to introduce six important themes in the letter to the Romans by following the flow of various sections and using "R-O-M-A-N-S" as an acronym. In addition, I have provided some brief applications for believers to consider as they learn to live in community with other believers and as they share the gospel with those around them. Here we will summarize the six themes of our acronym.

"R" stands for the "revelation of God's wrath," covering Romans 1:18–3:20. Paul's purpose in this section is to show that all—Jew and gentile alike—need the saving righteousness that God has revealed in Christ Jesus because all—Jew and gentile alike—are under the power of sin. Gentiles have denied the truth of God's power and eternal existence and have exchanged the glory of the Creator for created things. Jews have failed to obey the law and will not escape God's wrath on account of their ethnic heritage because God is impartial. Thus, despite certain advantages enjoyed by the Jews—mainly the possession of the law and circumcision—they too are under the power of sin. Paul concludes this section by concluding that no one will be justified by keeping the law (3:20).

"O" stands for the "*o*nly way to become righteous," covering Romans 3:21–4:25. Having established that all are under the power of sin and answerable to God's wrath, Paul returns to the opening theme of God's saving righteousness (1:17). He asserts in this section that God's saving righteousness has been revealed apart from the law, a saving righteousness that comes from God through faith in Jesus Christ for all who believe—Jew and gentile alike. Because all have fallen short of the glory of God and are justified by God's grace as a gift, there is no room for boasting. To illustrate how saving righteousness comes through faith in Christ for all, and to show the continuity between God's present work and the Old Testament, in Romans 4 Paul recounts the story of Abraham, who believed in God and was therefore counted righteous.

"M" stands for "*m*ade alive in Christ," covering Romans 5:1–8:17. Here Paul details the meaning and significance of God's saving righteousness. First, he describes how those who have been justified through faith in Christ have been transferred from the realm of sin to the realm of grace by becoming one with Christ, who is the Second Adam. Second, Paul highlights how God's saving righteousness does not lead to immorality because those who have been united to Christ have died to the power of sin and are now slaves of righteousness. Third, Paul argues that his gospel does not imply that there is something sinful about the law but shows the power of indwelling sin that prevents people from obeying the law despite their best efforts. Finally, those who have been united to Christ by faith now have the Spirit, who empowers them to do what they could not do otherwise when they were under the power of sin.

"A" stands for "*a*dopted for glory," covering Romans 8:18–30. Having become one with Christ by faith, believers can be confident that just as Christ was raised from the dead, they too will enjoy resurrection life. This hope of redemption is shared by all of creation, which will be freed from the effects of the fall when the children of God are brought into glory. The chapter concludes with one of the most majestic statements of God's love that assures believers that nothing can separate them from the love of God that is in Christ Jesus.

"N" stands for the "*n*ew lifestyle," covering Romans 12:1–15:13. Echoing the theme of worship found throughout the letter, this section begins with a general exhortation to believers to offer their bodies as living sacrifices and to be transformed by the renewal of their minds. Paul's emphasis in this section is on how believers are to treat one another. This emphasis was especially relevant (and is still relevant) as different and often opposing groups—namely, the Jews and the gentiles, the strong and the weak—came together under one household.

"S" stands for "*s*alvation according to God's mercy," covering Romans 9:1–11:36. In this section Paul addresses the relationship between God's righteousness and Israel's destiny. The fundamental question in chapters 9–11 is whether God has been faithful to Israel or whether he has rejected his people. Paul answers this question in three steps. First, he states the basic principle of election by which God created Israel and by which he is continuing to create a people for himself from the Jews and gentiles (9:1–29). Second, he states that the problem is not that God has been unfaithful to Israel but that Israel has refused to accept God's saving righteousness in Christ Jesus (9:30–10:21). Third, Paul affirms that God's call to Israel is irreversible and that after the full number of gentiles have been brought in, the full number of Israel will also receive mercy. The principle of election remains strong throughout these several chapters, highlighting that all—Jew and gentile alike—are saved on the basis of God's mercy. This is God's mysterious plan of salvation that has now been revealed through the gospel.

This thematic overview helps us better understand Paul's opening statement: "For I am not ashamed of the gospel, for it is the power of God for salvation for all who believe, to the Jew first and also to the Greek. For the righteousness of God is revealed in it from faith to faith, just as it is written, 'The righteous shall live by faith'" (1:16–17). All—Jew and gentile—were under the power of sin and deserved God's wrath. But in Jesus Christ—and only in Jesus Christ—God has made saving righteousness available to all who believe—Jew and gentile alike. Through faith we are made alive in Christ and dead to sin, and receive the gift of the Spirit, who empowers us to pursue righteousness. As recipients of the Spirit, Christians not only have the hope of glory but are also called to a new lifestyle. Such a high hope and calling are a result of God's mercy, expressed wondrously in God's salvation to all who trust in Jesus Christ.

For Further Study

I AM working on a more detailed commentary on Romans, which is not intended for scholars but for laypeople who want to work more closely with the text but still find some of the more technical commentaries inaccessible. I hope to make that commentary available by 2012.

For a readable, informed, and balanced treatment of Paul, I recommend Michael F. Bird, *Introducing Paul: The Man, His Mission, and His Message* (Downers Grove: InterVarsity, 2008). This book gives a brief but adequate survey of Paul's life and teaching.

There is no shortage of commentaries on Romans. For the purposes of advancing one step further in understanding the text and teaching of the letter, I recommend Frank J. Matera, *Romans*, Paideia (Grand Rapids: Baker Academic, 2010). Written by a respected New Testament scholar, this commentary is one of the most lucid expositions of Romans written to date. Its careful exegesis and interaction with old and new interpreters make it an excellent and ideal introductory commentary.

Douglas Moo has written a more technical commentary on Romans, but its density makes it less user friendly to the novice, especially for those unfamiliar with Greek. Nevertheless, his two other introductory works are very helpful for those who wish to learn more about Romans: *Romans*, NIV Application Commentary (Grand Rapids:

Zondervan, 2000); and *Encountering the Book of Romans: A Theological Survey*, Encountering Biblical Studies (Grand Rapids, Baker Academic, 2002).